Whole Numbers & Fractions

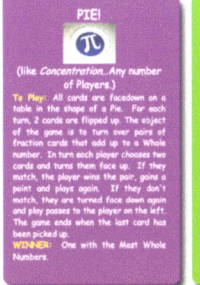

DEDICATION

This Book is dedicated to:

The Karner Blue Butterfly [1] in All Her Stages of Life,
And Ashley Namini, my Gorgeous Niece

Copyright

Blue Butterfly Books Math & Science Activities are Published by:

Blue Butterfly Books ™
Victoria BC
Canada V8S 4H9
www.ButterflyBooks.ca

Copyright ©, Sheila M. Hynes, *Blue Butterfly Books* ™
All rights reserved. This book or parts thereof may not be reproduced in any form without permission.   Please visit our website for more information: www.butterflybooks.ca

ISBN-13: 978-0-9920530-1-7
ISBN-10: 0992053013

For other affordable, downloadable and printable Math and Science Games, feel free to visit:
www.math-lessons.ca
www.science-lessons.ca
Printed in the USA

Team Members for this Publication:
Editor: Sheila M. Hynes, *BA Hons, MES, York*
Contributor: Brian Stocker, *BA, MA, Santa Monica*
Contributor: D. A. Stocker, *BA, M Ed, Victoria*
Contributor: Dr. G.A. Stocker, *DDS, Toronto*

Copyright © 2013, by *Blue Butterfly Books* ™, Sheila M. Hynes. ALL RIGHTS RESERVED.
No part of this book may be reproduced or transferred in any form or by any means, graphic, electronic, or mechanical, including photocopying, recording, web distribution, taping, or by any information storage retrieval system, without the written permission of the author.

Notice: *Blue Butterfly Books* makes every reasonable effort to obtain from reliable sources accurate, complete, and timely information about the tests covered in this book. Nevertheless, changes can be made in the tests or the administration of the tests at any time, and *Blue Butterfly Books* makes no representations or warranties of any kind, expressed or implied, about the completeness, accuracy, reliability, suitability or availability with respect to the information contained in this document for any purpose. Any reliance you place on such information is therefore strictly at your own risk.

The author(s) shall not be liable for any loss incurred as a consequence of the use and application, directly or indirectly, of any information presented in this work. Sold with the understanding, the author is not engaged in rendering professional services or advice. If advice or expert assistance is required, the services of a competent professional should be sought.

The company, product and service names used in this book are for identification purposes only. All trademarks and registered trademarks are the property of their respective owners. *Blue Butterfly Books* is not affiliate with any educational institution.

Table of Contents

Dedication..3

Copyright..4

Table of Contents...7

Sustainability and Eco-Responsibility...8

Customization and White Label Service..9

Other Books, Study Guides, and Activities..10

Let's Begin!...11

Teachers' Resources Pages..12

Deck Cover Card...14

Instructions Cards..19

Playing Cards..21

Deck Tuck Box..51

Congratulations!..53

Endnotes...54

Notes..55

Sustainability and Eco-Responsibility

Here at *Blue Butterfly Books*, trees are valuable to Mother Earth and the health and wellbeing of everyone. Minimizing our ecological footprint and effect on the environment, we choose *Create Space*, an eco-responsible printing company.

Electronic routing of our books reduces greenhouse gas emissions, worldwide. When a book order is received, the order is filled at the printing location closest to the client. Using environmentally friendly publishing technology, of the *Espresso* book printing machine, *Blue Butterfly Books* are printed as they are requested, saving thousands of books, and trees over time. This process offers the stable and viable alternative keeping healthy sustainability of our environment. All paper is acid-free, and interior paper stock is made from 30% post-consumer waste recycled material.

Safe for children, *Create Space* also verifies the materials used in the print process are all CPSIA-compliant.

By purchasing this *Blue Butterfly Book*, you have supported Full Recovery and Preservation of The Karner Blue Butterfly. Our logo is the Karner Blue Butterfly, *Lycaeides melissa samuelis*, a rare and beautiful butterfly species whose only flower for propogation is the blue lupin flower. The Karner Butterfly is mostly found in the Great Lakes Region of the U.S.A. Recovery planning is in action, for the return of Karner Blue in Canada led by the National Recovery Strategy. The recovery goals and objectives are aimed at recreating suitable habitats for the butterfly and encourage the growth of blue lupines - the butterfly's natural ideal habitat.

For more info on the Karner Blue Butterfly feel free to visit:

http://www.albanypinebush.org/conservation/wildlife-management/karner-blue-butterfly-recovery

http://www.wiltonpreserve.org/conservation/karner-blue-butterfly.

http://www.natureconservancy.ca/en/what-we-do/resource-centre/featured-species/karner_blue.html.

Customization and White Label Service

Have your logo and school name on the front cover in a special edition produced for you're your school or institution; Visit: www.ButterflyBooks.ca

Or Feel Free to Contact us for details at:
info@ButterflyBooks.ca

Other Books, Study Guides, and Activities

Blue Butterfly Books™ also has:

Study Guides for High School and College Entrance in All Disciplines:
www.ButterflyBooks.ca, and;

Math and Science Activites
For our On-Line Downloadable Games and Free Lesson Plans:
www.math-lessons.ca
www.science-lessons.ca

Let's Begin!

Have Fun Learning Whole Numbers & Fractions!

This Set of Math Cards is designed to achieve Learning Standard Requirements for Grade Levels 4-6 Mathematics and Communication. They are printed to be "Cut-Out" and made into a 63-Card Playing Deck.

Deck Includes: 1 Deck Cover Card, 4 Instruction Cards, 55 Fraction Playing Cards and 3 Wild Cards. 3 Wildcards can be used for any card during play. HAVE FUN!

4 Learning Games are included:
1. Go Figure! (like *Go Fish!*)
2. Pie! (like *Concentration*)
3. Matrix!
4. Calculator! (like *Jeopardy*)

Games *Go Figure!* And *Pie!* are simple comprehension games; while *Calculator!* and *Matrix!* are more challenging.

Brain Developing:
- ✓ Spacial Functioning
- ✓ Memory
- ✓ Cognition
- ✓ Coordination

Mathematics Learning Objectives:
- ✓ Levels 4-6 Mathematics and Communication
- ✓ Whole Numbers and Fractions, Adding, Subtraction, Multiplication, Reasoning, memory, problem solving, and communication

Communication:
- ✓ Listening and observation skills and strategies to gain understanding
- ✓ Strategies for focusing attention and interpreting information
- ✓ Understanding, analyzing, synthesizing, or evaluating information
- ✓ Communication skills and strategies to interact/work effectively with others
- ✓ Working collaboratively, solve problems, and perform tasks.

Teacher's Resources Page

The following are Notes for Teachers corresponding to the 4 Instructions Deck Cards:

Pie
(like *Concentration*…Any number of Players.)

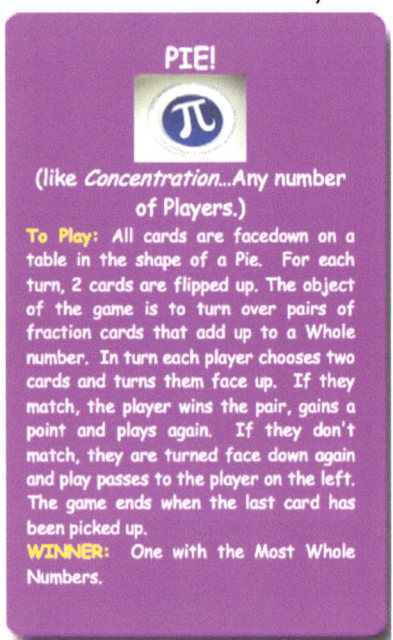

To Play: All cards are placed facedown on a table in the shape of a Pie. For each turn, 2 cards are flipped up. The object of the game is to turn over pairs that add up to a Whole Number. In turn, each player chooses two cards and turns them face up. If they match, the player wins the pair, gains a point and plays again. If they don't match, they are turned face down again and the play passes to the player on the left. The game ends when the last card has been picked up.

WINNER: One with the Most Whole Numbers.

Go Figure!
(Like *Go Fish!*)

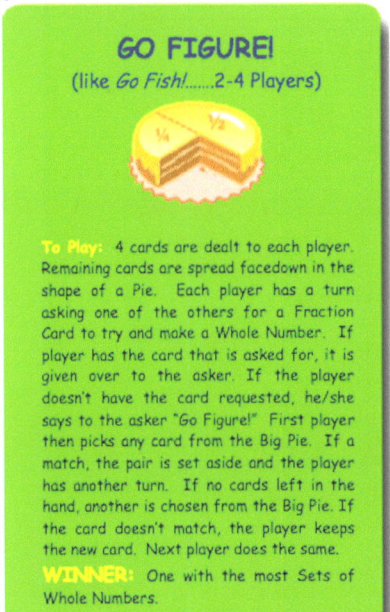

To Play: 4 Cards are dealt to each player. The remaining cards are spread facedown in the shape of a Pie.

Each player has a turn asking one of the others for a Fraction Card to try and make a Whole Number. If the player has the card that is asked for, it is given over to the asker. If the player doesn't have the card requested, he/ she says to the asker "Go Figure!" The First player then picks any card from the Big Pie. If a match, the pair is set aside and the player has another turn. If threre are no cards left in the hand, another is chosen from the Big Pie. If it is a match, the pair is set aside and the player has another turn. If there are no cards left in the hand, another is chosen from the Big Pie. If the card doesn't match, the player keeps the new card. The next player does the same.

WINNER: One with the Most Sets of Whole Numbers.

MATRIX!

To Play: Neutral Calculators are randomly decided. (An actual calculator can be used by a few to periodically confirm answers to other Learners). Average 1 Calculator for every 4 Learners in a group. All cards are dealt to as many players as there are in a group. The number of cards to each player does not have to be even. (If there are 15 players, each player has 3 cards, though 10 of the 15 players have 4 cards. If there are 20 players, each player has 2 cards, though 15 players have 3.) Each player adds his or her card(s) together secretly. Each player walks the room randomly, looking for another player whose Total Card(s) equal the completion of his or her Fraction Total to make a Whole Number. Those players then join together to form a Team. Each Team then walks the room once again, looking for another Team whose Total Card(s) equal to the completion of their Fraction Total to make a Whole Number. Eg. Gabrielle has 1/4; Ryan has 9/12. Together, they equal 12/12 or 1. Gabrielle and Ryan, Together as a Team, must then find another Team equaling their Whole Number 1; And So on.

WINNER: Team when added together, equals the Highest Whole Number, is The Winner.

Calculator: (*like* Jeopardy!)

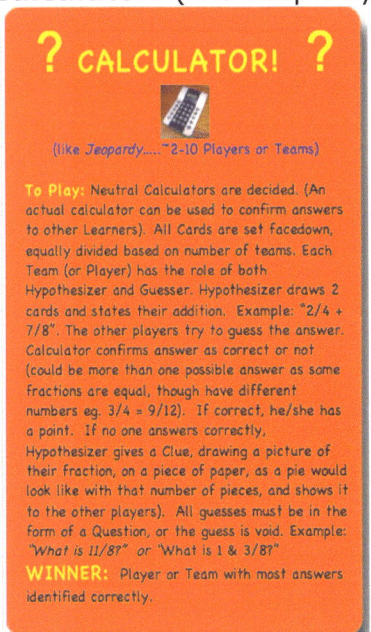

To Play: Neutral Calculators are decided. (An actual calculator can be used to confirm answers to other Learners). All Cards are set facedown, equally divided, based on the number of teams. Each Team (or Player) has the role of both Hypothesizer and Guesser. The Hypothesizer draws 2 cards and states their addition. Example: "2/4 + 7/8". The other players try to guess the answer. The Calculator confirms if the answer is correct or not (there could be more than one possible answer as some fractions are equal, though have different numbers eg. 3/4 = 9/12). If correct, he/she has a point. If no one answers correctly, the Hypothesizer gives a Clue, drawing a picture of their fraction, on a piece of paper - as a pie would look like with that number of pieces, and shows it to the other players). All guesses must be in the form of a Question, or the guess is void. Example: "What is 11/8?" or "What is 1 & 3/8?"

WINNER: Player or Team with most answers identified correctly.

FRACTIONS

The word "fraction" is from the Latin *fractus*, meaning *broken*. A fraction is a number that represents part of a whole.

Common fractions are also called vulgars, meaning *commonplace*. They have a numerator and a denominator, the numerator representing a number of parts and the denominator telling how many of those parts make up a whole. An example is 3/4 in which the numerator, 3, tells us that the fraction represents 3 parts, and the denominator, 4, tells us that 4 parts, make up a whole.

The earliest fractions were reciprocals of integers, symbols representing one half, one third, one quarter, and so on. The numbers that we now call "decimals", were at one time, called "decimal fractions".

All Reference Material: Wikipedia.com. See EndNotes.

The Next pages are your Deck Cover Card, followed by Instruction Cards, Playing Cards, Wildcards and a Tuck Box to keep all your cards in for storage.

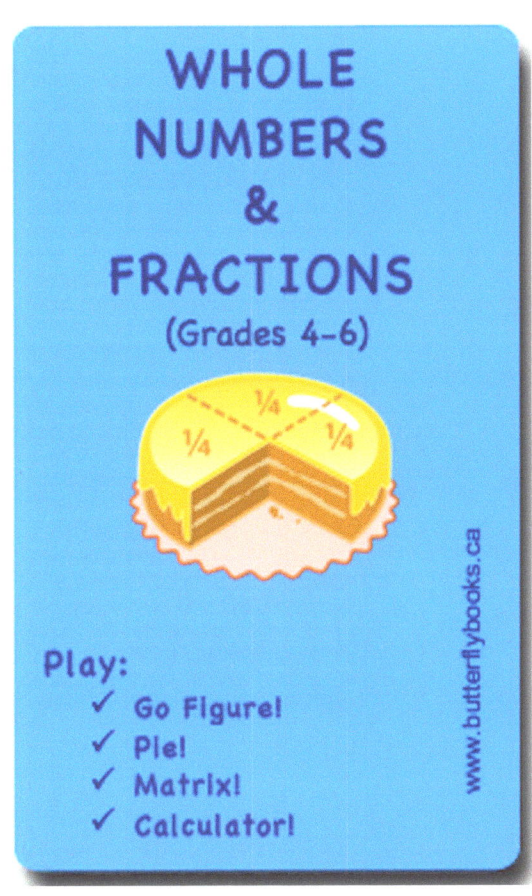

GO FIGURE!
(like *Go Fish!*........2-4 Players)

To Play: 4 cards are dealt to each player. Remaining cards are spread facedown in the shape of a Pie. Each player has a turn asking one of the others for a Fraction Card to try and make a Whole Number. If player has the card that is asked for, it is given over to the asker. If the player doesn't have the card requested, he/she says to the asker "Go Figure!" First player then picks any card from the Big Pie. If a match, the pair is set aside and the player has another turn. If no cards left in the hand, another is chosen from the Big Pie. If the card doesn't match, the player keeps the new card. Next player does the same.
WINNER: One with the most Sets of Whole Numbers.

PIE!

(like *Concentration*...Any number of Players.)

To Play: All cards are facedown on a table in the shape of a Pie. For each turn, 2 cards are flipped up. The object of the game is to turn over pairs of fraction cards that add up to a Whole number. In turn each player chooses two cards and turns them face up. If they match, the player wins the pair, gains a point and plays again. If they don't match, they are turned face down again and play passes to the player on the left. The game ends when the last card has been picked up.
WINNER: One with the Most Whole Numbers.

? CALCULATOR! ?

(like *Jeopardy*.....~2-10 Players or Teams)

To Play: Neutral Calculators are decided. (An actual calculator can be used to confirm answers to other Learners). All Cards are set facedown, equally divided based on number of teams. Each Team (or Player) has the role of both Hypothesizer and Guesser. Hypothesizer draws 2 cards and states their addition. Example: "2/4 + 7/8". The other players try to guess the answer. Calculator confirms answer as correct or not (could be more than one possible answer as some fractions are equal, though have different numbers eg. 3/4 = 9/12). If correct, he/she has a point. If no one answers correctly, Hypothesizer gives a Clue, drawing a picture of their fraction, on a piece of paper, as a pie would look like with that number of pieces, and shows it to the other players). All guesses must be in the form of a Question, or the guess is void. Example: "What is 11/8?" or "What is 1 & 3/8?"
WINNER: Player or Team with most answers identified correctly.

MATRIX!

To Play: Neutral Calculators are randomly decided. (An actual calculator can be used by a few to periodically confirm answers to other Learners). Average 1 Calculator for every 4 Learners in a group. All cards dealt to as many players as there are in a group. Number of cards to each player does not have to be even. (If 15 players, each has 3 cards, though 10 of the 15 players have 4 cards. If 20 players, each has 2 cards, though 15 players have 3.) Each player adds his or her card(s) together secretly. Each player walks the room randomly, looking for another player whose Total Card(s) equal the completion of *his or her* Fraction Total to make a Whole Number. Those players then join together to form a Team. Each Team then walks the room once again, looking for another Team whose Total Card(s) equals to the completion of *their* Fraction Total to make a Whole Number. Eg. Gabrielle has 1/4; Ryan has 9/12. Together, they equal 12/12 or 1. Gabrielle and Ryan, Together as a Team, must then find another Team equaling their Whole Number 1; And So on.
WINNER: Team when added together, equals the Highest Whole Number.

$$\frac{1}{10}$$ $$\frac{2}{10}$$

$$\frac{3}{10}$$ $$\frac{4}{10}$$

$$\frac{5}{10}$$

$$\frac{6}{10}$$

$$\frac{7}{10}$$

$$\frac{8}{10}$$

$$\frac{9}{10} \qquad \frac{10}{10}$$

$$\frac{1}{9} \qquad \frac{2}{9}$$

$$\frac{3}{9}\qquad \frac{4}{9}$$

$$\frac{5}{9}\qquad \frac{6}{9}$$

$$\frac{7}{9}$$

$$\frac{8}{9}$$

$$\frac{9}{9}$$

$$\frac{1}{8}$$

$$\frac{2}{8} \quad \frac{3}{8}$$

$$\frac{4}{8} \quad \frac{5}{8}$$

$$\frac{6}{8}$$

$$\frac{7}{8}$$

$$\frac{8}{8}$$

$$\frac{1}{7}$$

$$\frac{2}{7} \quad \frac{3}{7}$$

$$\frac{4}{7} \quad \frac{5}{7}$$

$$\frac{6}{7}$$

$$\frac{7}{7}$$

$$\frac{1}{6}$$

$$\frac{2}{6}$$

$$\frac{3}{6} \quad \frac{4}{6}$$

$$\frac{5}{6} \quad \frac{6}{6}$$

40

$$\frac{1}{5} \quad \frac{2}{5}$$

$$\frac{3}{5} \quad \frac{4}{5}$$

$$\frac{5}{5} \quad \frac{1}{4}$$

$$\frac{2}{4} \quad \frac{3}{4}$$

$$\frac{4}{4} \quad \frac{1}{3}$$

$$\frac{2}{3} \quad \frac{3}{3}$$

$$\frac{1}{2}$$

$$\frac{2}{2}$$

$$\frac{1}{1}$$

WILDCARD

WILDCARD   WILDCARD

Whole Numbers & Fractions

Blue Butterfly Books™

www.ButterflyBooks.ca

- With scissors, cut around outside.
- Make folds along all inner lines.
- Glue far-left side edge < to > far-right side edge (1.6 cm each side).
- Glue bottom-left side upward (1 cm)

CONGRATULATIONS!

You made it!! You have made yourself a Deck of Cards that can improve your Learning Fractions in Math for Hours and Hours of Fun. Thank you for playing with

Blue Butterfly Books™ in our mandate to make Learning Math easy and fun!

ENDNOTES:

From p. 13 Instruction Cards:

1. Blue Butterfly. In Microsoft Clipart. Retrieved October 15, 2013 from: http://office.microsoft.com/en-CA/images/results.aspx?qu=blue%20butterfly&ex=2#ai:MP900314069|

2. Cake_fractions.svg. In Wikipedia. Retrieved February 22, 2009 from: http://en.wikipedia.org/wiki/Fractions

3. Flower-of-Life-small.svg. In Wikipedia. Retrieved October 15, 2013 from: http://en.wikipedia.org/wiki/Flower_of_life304px

Text where noted below is used under the Creative Commons Attributions Attribution-Share Alike 3.0 License.

http://en.wikipedia.org/wiki/Wikipedia: Text_of_Creative_Commons_Attribution-ShareAlike_3.0_Unported_ License

NOTES

www.ingramcontent.com/pod-product-compliance
Lightning Source LLC
LaVergne TN
LVHW072113070426
835510LV00002B/32